The Youngest Marcher

The Story of Audrey Faye Hendricks,
a Young Civil Rights Activist

Cynthia Levinson

illustrated by

Vanessa Brantley Newton

atheneum

ATHENEUM BOOKS FOR YOUNG READERS

New York   London   Toronto   Sydney   New Delhi

To Jan Hendricks Fuller, to the memory of Audrey Faye Hendricks,
and to the women and girls of the civil rights movement —C. L.

To the Charleston Nine and Sharonda Singleton Coleman's family —V. B. N.

ATHENEUM BOOKS FOR YOUNG READERS
An imprint of Simon & Schuster Children's Publishing Division
1230 Avenue of the Americas, New York, New York 10020
Text copyright © 2017 by Cynthia Levinson
Illustrations copyright © 2017 by Vanessa Brantley Newton
Photograph of Audrey Faye Hendricks on p. 36 copyright © 1965 by
Center Street Elementary School. All rights reserved. Reprinted by permission of
Jan Hendricks Fuller.
All rights reserved, including the right of reproduction in whole or in part
in any form.
ATHENEUM BOOKS FOR YOUNG READERS is a registered trademark of
Simon & Schuster, Inc.
Atheneum logo is a trademark of Simon & Schuster, Inc.
For information about special discounts for bulk purchases, please contact
Simon & Schuster Special Sales at
1-866-506-1949 or business@simonandschuster.com.
The Simon & Schuster Speakers Bureau can bring authors to your live event.
For more information or to book an event, contact the Simon & Schuster
Speakers Bureau at 1-866-248-3049 or visit our website at
www.simonspeakers.com.
Book design by Ann Bobco
The text for this book is set in Souvenir Std.
The illustrations for this book are rendered in digital collage.
Manufactured in China
0217 SCP
10 9 8 7 6 5 4 3 2
Library of Congress Cataloging-in-Publication Data
Names: Levinson, Cynthia. | Brantley-Newton, Vanessa, illustrator.
Title: The youngest marcher : the story of Audrey Faye Hendricks, a young civil
rights activist / Cynthia Levinson ; illustrated by Vanessa Brantley Newton.
Description: First edition. | New York : Atheneum Books
for Young Readers, an imprint of Simon & Schuster Children's Pub. Division,
2017.
Identifiers: LCCN 2013032438
ISBN 978-1-4814-0070-1
ISBN 978-1-4814-0071-8 (eBook)
Subjects: LCSH: Hendricks, Audrey Faye—Juvenile
literature. | African American civil rights workers—
Alabama—Birmingham—Biography—Juvenile literature. | Civil rights
workers—Alabama—Birmingham—Biography—Juvenile literature. |
African Americans—Civil rights—Alabama—Birmingham—History—
20th century—Juvenile literature. | Civil rights movements—Alabama—
Birmingham—History—20th century—Juvenile literature. | Birmingham
(Ala.)—Race relations—Juvenile literature. | Birmingham (Ala.)—
Biography—Juvenile literature.
Classification: LCC F334.B653 H465 2017 | DDC 323.092—dc23
LC record available at http://lccn.loc.gov/2013032438

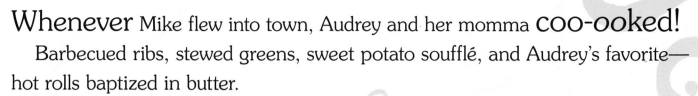

Whenever Mike flew into town, Audrey and her momma coo-ooked!
Barbecued ribs, stewed greens, sweet potato soufflé, and Audrey's favorite—
hot rolls baptized in butter.

Other folks knew Mike as Martin or Dr. King. The Hendrickses used his nickname. They did the same with other ministers too— like Fred Shuttlesworth and Jim Bevel.

After Mike blessed the feast, Momma expected Audrey to keep still during supper. But when grown-ups talked about wiping out the segregation laws that kept black and white people apart in Birmingham, she just had to speak up. Audrey intended to go places and do things like anybody else.

I want to eat my ice cream *inside* Newberry's!

I want to sit *downstairs* at the Alabama!

I *don't* want hand-me-down schoolbooks!

But stools at the counter, plush movie theater seats, books so fresh they'd crackle when you open them— those were for white children.

Hush! hissed Momma. Nine-year-old children should not speak in front of company, especially ministers like Mike, Fred, and Jim, who were bringing dreams of justice.

Audrey knew all about segregation.

She knew to pay the driver
at the front of the bus,
then step off and walk
around to the back door.

Drink from the fountain
with the dirty bowl and
warm water.

Use the freight elevator at
department stores downtown.

Front-row seats, cool water, elevators with white-gloved operators—
laws said those were for white folks.

Every Monday night, Audrey and her momma and daddy
and her aunts, uncles, and cousins joined neighbors and
friends at Fred's church for worship, fellowship, and
testimony. She sang and swayed along with the
Movement Choir, her voice spirited and
spiritual. "Black and white toge-*e*-ther, we
shall overcome." For once, she didn't
have to keep still.

Then came testimonies.

White store owners *won't* hire me!

Ku Kluxers *chased* me!

Policemen *called* me names!

The hateful stories made Audrey squirm. She tried to tell her momma, *That's not right!*

Shhh!

How could Momma expect her to hush? She had to make things right. But what could she do?

When Mike visited Fred's church, thousands of people crowded around her to hear him preach. In a voice as taut as steel cables, as smooth as glass, he intoned, "[S]egregation . . . is morally wrong and sinful." That's true! Fired up, Audrey sat taller.

"An unjust law is no law at all," he proclaimed. Audrey had listened to Mike explain his plan at her supper table and knew what he meant. If a law is unjust, disobey it.

Sit down *inside* Newberry's!

Picket those white stores!

March to protest those unfair laws!
Why, even marching was against the law.

Then, get arrested.

"Fill the jails!" Mike exclaimed. Fill Birmingham's jails so full that policemen can't squeeze in one more person. Pack cells so tight that police will have to quit arresting people for demanding their rights.

Audrey just knew Mike's plan would work. She twisted in her pew to see which grown-ups would walk down the aisle, volunteer for jail. But they mostly stayed put, eyes staring at their feet, hands on their knees. Feet, hands, and knees didn't move.

"Fill the jails," Mike pleaded, meeting after meeting.

But heads shook. All around her, Audrey heard, *No, best not break those segregation laws.*

Boss man will *fire* me!
Landlord will *evict* me!
Policemen will *beat* me!

If nobody protested, Mike's plan would fail. Police could keep arresting anyone, anytime, for anything, forever. Audrey would never be able to go places and do things like everybody else.

One night, Jim announced
a new idea. If grown-ups won't
do it, fill the jails...with children!

Audrey leaped to her feet.
"I want to go to jail," she declared.
Momma looked deep and saw that
Audrey's eyes begged, *Please*.
"Okay," Momma said.
Audrey strutted down that aisle.
She was going to **j-a-*a*-il**!

Two mornings later, she put on a fresh-pressed pinafore and shiny Mary Janes with turned-down socks. Protesters got to look nice. In the meantime, her daddy bought her a game to help her pass the time in jail.

Her momma and daddy took her by Center Street Elementary to tell her teacher she'd be absent, maybe for a whole week. Miss Wills wrapped her arms around her. Audrey knew she was proud of her.

She said good-bye to her grandparents. "You'll be fine," her grandmother said. She knew Audrey would be brave. So did Audrey.

Then her momma and daddy drove her to Sixteenth Street Baptist Church where the children were gathering.

Even before she reached the door, Audrey heard loud voices chanting freedom songs.

Inside, hundreds of big kids called out to friends and crowded around signs for their high schools. PARKER. CARVER. Her head swiveled. Where was the sign for Center Street Elementary?

She was the only protester from her school, the youngest child in the whole church, and she knew no one.

Audrey huddled by her parents in the basement.

Can a Man LOVE GOD and Hate his brother?

Justice for All

SEGREGATION is SIN

SEGREGATION is SIN

Free NOW

But when Jim lined her up with the others, two by two, and the doors swung open, Audrey straightened up. She was going to break a law and go to jail to help make things right.

Clutching a protest sign in one hand and her game in the other, Audrey marched out the door. She stomped and sang, "Ain't gonna le-e-t nobody turn me 'round, turn me 'round, turn me 'round."

Half a block from the church, a white policeman stopped Audrey.
He pointed toward a police van.

Sentence: one week in juvenile hall.

A matron locked Audrey into
a dayroom with two dozen
other girls—all older, all bigger,
all strangers. Audrey sat down,
alone, and slipped the cover
off her game.

"I told you to sit down!" the matron yelled. Audrey jumped. She didn't remember standing up.

The matron dragged her to a dark, empty room. "When I tell you something, you do it," she commanded. "Or I'll leave you here."

Trembling, Audrey quietly followed the matron
back to the dayroom, put away her game, lay
down her head, and cried. Jail was harder than
she'd thought, and she wasn't fine, after all.

By evening, Audrey was hungry and tired.
For dinner—soupy, oily, tasteless grits. At night—
a bare mattress with one thin sheet for a cover.

The next morning, uh-oh—no fresh underwear,
no clean pinafore, no toothbrush.

Audrey and her cell mates were let outdoors into an empty, concrete pen surrounded by high prison walls. The older girls talked together.

Audrey wondered what her classmates were doing. Miss Wills would be keeping them busy.

On another day, Audrey was sent to a huge room and told to sit in a chair that was so high, her feet dangled above the floor. Four white men glared at her. She'd never talked to a white man before.

"Are you against America?" one demanded to know.

"No, sir," she answered politely.

"What do you talk about at those meetings?" another asked.

"Our freedom."

"Why did you march?"

"To go places and do things like anybody else." What was wrong with that?

Every mealtime, Audrey stared at greasy grits. She could barely spoon them into her mouth, let alone swallow them. Every night, the cot's wire springs jabbed.

Every morning, she had nothing to do but sit alone with her game.

In the afternoons, though, more kids crowded into the dayroom.

Some days, many of them arrived sopping wet. A girl explained that
firemen aimed powerful hoses at the children. Surging water
spun them off their feet and down the street.

They got up and kept marching, anyway—until they too were sent to jail.

By Audrey's fifth day in detention, the police couldn't squeeze in one more person.

"We filled up all the rooms! We filled up all the rooms!" Audrey practically jumped up and down, she was so proud!

We filled up all the rooms

Watching television in the dayroom, she saw black people stroll straight into stores and restaurants like they belonged there. No one else could be sent to jail. Everything had changed.

After seven days, Audrey went home. Her momma and daddy wrapped their arms tight around her, washed the jail off her, and for dinner . . .

hot rolls, baptized in butter!

Two months later, the City of Birmingham wiped segregation laws clean off the books. Audrey licked her spoon clean at Newberry's counter, like everybody else.

Black and white together, like we belong.

AUTHOR'S NOTE

Audrey Faye Hendricks

Every day Audrey Faye Hendricks spent in jail, her mother, Lola, called someone she knew there to make sure her daughter was safe. The day after her release, Audrey returned to Miss Wills's class. She didn't tell her classmates about marching or jail, though.

"It didn't dawn on me that it was a big deal," she said.

But it was. Audrey was one of more than three thousand children who were arrested in Birmingham, Alabama, in May 1963. The Children's March, which was planned by Reverend James Bevel, Reverend Fred Shuttlesworth, and Dr. Martin Luther King Jr., affected not only Birmingham but America. That summer, young people held protests in nearly two hundred cities. President John F. Kennedy spoke on television about prejudice and sent a civil rights bill to Congress. On August 28, about 250,000 people marched in Washington, D.C., to hear Dr. King preach about his dreams of freedom.

I had the honor of talking with Audrey in her home, where she grew up. She showed me the table at which Dr. King blessed their meals and the upright piano where she practiced singing civil rights songs, including "Ain't Gonna Let Nobody Turn Me 'Round."

Audrey told me that she remained an activist afterward. She volunteered to integrate a high school, enrolling as one of its first black students. "It took a while for whites and blacks to work together," she said. "But it was what we fought for."

After graduating from college and working in Dallas, Texas, Audrey returned to Birmingham where she taught preschool and led Head Start programs. Years later, she earned a graduate degree researching women, like her mother and herself, who were involved in the civil rights movement. Schools around the country invited her to speak about her experience as the youngest known marcher.

Nicknamed the "Civil Rights Queen," Audrey Faye Hendricks died in 2009.

"What a difference the Children's March has made in this nation."
—Audrey Faye Hendricks, January 12, 2008

TIME LINE

1944: Birmingham, Alabama, adopted racial segregation ordinances that declared it "unlawful to conduct a restaurant . . . at which white and colored people are served in the same room . . . [and] for a negro and a white person to play together."

June 4, 1956: Reverend Fred Shuttlesworth began holding weekly church meetings to plan integration of schools and facilities in Birmingham.

January 1963: Reverend Shuttlesworth urged Dr. Martin Luther King Jr. to come to Birmingham to help the civil rights movement there.

April 1963: Dr. King discussed strategies with many people, including the Hendrickses. He called for nightly mass meetings and asked volunteers to picket and sit in at segregated stores and restaurants so they would be arrested and fill the jails. Few adults volunteered.

April 29, 1963: Reverend James Bevel proposed that children march and go to jail.

May 2–7, 1963: The Children's March resulted in the arrests of 3,000–4,000 young people, filling the jails. Audrey Faye Hendricks, the youngest known marcher, was arrested on the first day.

June 19, 1963: President John F. Kennedy submitted a civil rights bill to Congress.

July 23, 1963: Birmingham rescinded its segregation ordinances.

August 28, 1963: Civil rights activists held the March on Washington for jobs and freedom.

September 15, 1963: Four black girls were killed by a bomb at the Sixteenth Street Baptist Church.

July 2, 1964: Congress passed the Civil Rights Act of 1964.

RECIPE

When Audrey and her sister, Jan Hendricks Fuller, grew up, they wanted to make their mother's hot rolls baptized in butter. But Mrs. Hendricks never wrote down her recipe. So they experimented with many recipes and decided that this one tastes just right. Although I never tasted their mother's rolls, I make these for my family, and we agree that they taste just right! Be sure that a grown-up helps you when you make them for your family.

HOT ROLLS BAPTIZED IN BUTTER

Makes about 25 to 30 rolls

INGREDIENTS:

5 tablespoons warm water

1 package yeast

5 cups flour, plus a little extra

½ teaspoon double-acting baking soda

2 tablespoons sugar

5 teaspoons baking powder

1 teaspoon salt

1 cup shortening

2 cups whole buttermilk

½ cup butter, softened

DIRECTIONS:

1. Turn on the oven to 400° F.

2. Pour the warm water into a small bowl. Sprinkle the yeast on top. Set aside.

3. Sift 5 cups of flour and the baking soda, sugar, baking powder, and salt into a large bowl. Place the shortening on top. With your fingers, cut the shortening into the dry ingredients until the dough is mixed up and crumbly.

4. Make a well in the middle of the dough. Slowly pour in the water-and-yeast mixture and the buttermilk. Stir ingredients together with a wooden spoon until the dough is sticky.

5. Spread a thin layer of the extra flour onto a large cutting board. Dump the dough onto the flour, turn it over, and knead it for a few minutes. Spread the dough with your fingers into a circle about ¾ inch thick.

6. Dip a biscuit cutter in flour and cut out biscuits until you've used up the dough. Dip the top of each biscuit in the softened butter and place on a baking sheet, butter side up.

7. Bake the biscuits for 15 to 20 minutes until they're golden brown. Anoint with more butter and enjoy!

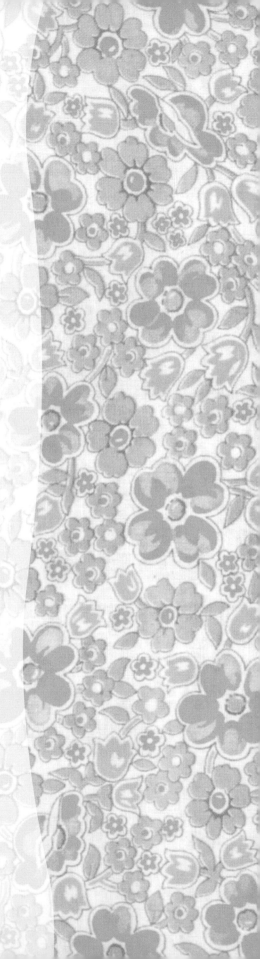

SOURCES

The Birmingham Civil Rights Institute (BCRI) has interviewed hundreds of local civil rights activists. Transcriptions of these interviews are available through the Institute's Archives. BCRI also maintains an informative website at bcri.org/index.html.

Books for young readers on or containing information about events in Birmingham include:

Brimner, Larry Dane. *Black & White: The Confrontation between Reverend Fred L. Shuttlesworth and Eugene "Bull" Connor.* Honesdale: Calkins Creek, 2011.

Levine, Ellen S. *Freedom's Children: Young Civil Rights Activists Tell Their Own Stories.* New York: Puffin Books, 1993.

Mayer, Robert H. *When the Children Marched: The Birmingham Civil Rights Movement.* Berkeley Heights: Enslow Publishers, 2008.

McWhorter, Diane. *A Dream of Freedom: The Civil Rights Movement from 1954 to 1968.* New York: Scholastic, 2004.

Rochelle, Belinda. *Witnesses to Freedom: Young People Who Fought for Civil Rights.* New York: Puffin Books, 1993.

I am especially grateful to Audrey Faye Hendricks and Jan Hendricks Fuller for talking with me about their experiences. My book for older readers, *We've Got a Job: The 1963 Birmingham Children's March*, provides a fuller story of the involvement of Audrey and three other young activists in the Children's March.